Santa Barbara
A California Coastal Town

Written by Jane Centofante

Illustrated by Mike West

Boardwalk Press
Manhattan Beach 2014

Santa Barbara
A California Coastal Town

First Edition

Text ©2014 by Jane Centofante
Artwork ©2014 by Mike West
All rights reserved. No part of this publication may be reproduced without the written permission of the publisher. Brand names and trademarks of products mentioned in this book are the property of their registered owners.

Library of Congress Control Number 2014912427
ISBN 978-0-692-25407-3
Published by Boardwalk Press
Printed and bound in the United States of America
boardwalkpress.com

10 9 8 7 6 5 4 3 2 1

Book design: Linda Warren, Studio Deluxe

"In the fairest of valleys, on the tranquilest shore,
 By mountains walled in, and an ocean before,
 With her brow on the hills, and her feet to the sea,
 Santa Barbara stands—the Queen that's to be."

– E.W. TUCKER (1883)

Set like a priceless jewel in the crown, Santa Barbara perches on the central California coast, its lustrous facets sparkling aside the Pacific Ocean. Once a diamond in the rough where rugged hills spilled down onto sandy dunes, this region was first inhabited by the native Chumash Indians. As Spanish explorers and missionaries arrived, they brought new customs and traditions and established one of the town's most cherished gems, the Santa Barbara Mission. Today, it is a unique city that still possesses the charm of its old Spanish days, while showcasing the sophistication of a modern and vibrant cultural center. Take a walk through this California coastal town and its surrounding enclaves, each of them places to be discovered and treasured. Santa Barbara truly is California royalty.

Blooming jacarandas grace State Street... along with signs of the time

La Arcada — a place to shop and sun for tourists and turtles alike

Red Tile City

Guardian of the city since 1782,
El Presidio de Santa Bárbara still echoes California history

Jumping for joy at Stearns Wharf!

Sandpipers and sunbathers flock to a favorite beachfront grill

Cabrillo sailing the blue in 1452

East Beach has been digging volleyball in the sand since the 1960s

Old Spanish Days remember the city's multi-cultural heritage…

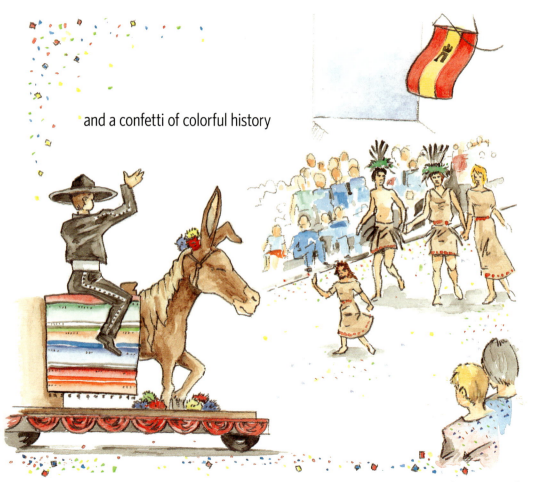

and a confetti of colorful history

Día de los Muertos celebrates sacred tradition at the 1827 Casa de la Guerra

The stately 1929 Courthouse continues to serve justice and artful civic pride

Time travel to another era at the train depot with a stop at a classic diner

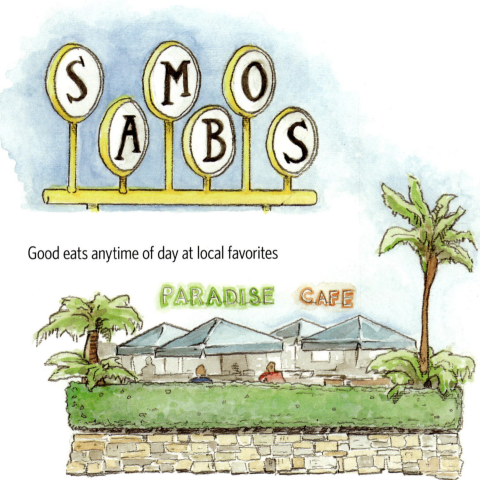

Good eats anytime of day at local favorites

McConnell's SINCE 1949
FINE ICE CREAMS

A tree grows in Santa Barbara —

the city's own Moreton Bay Fig planted roots in 1877

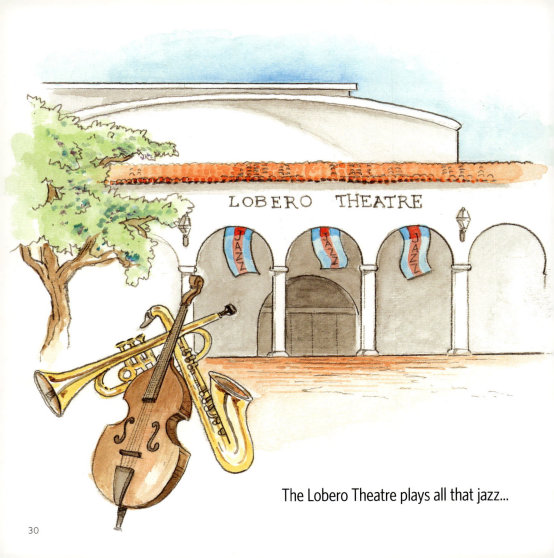
The Lobero Theatre plays all that jazz...

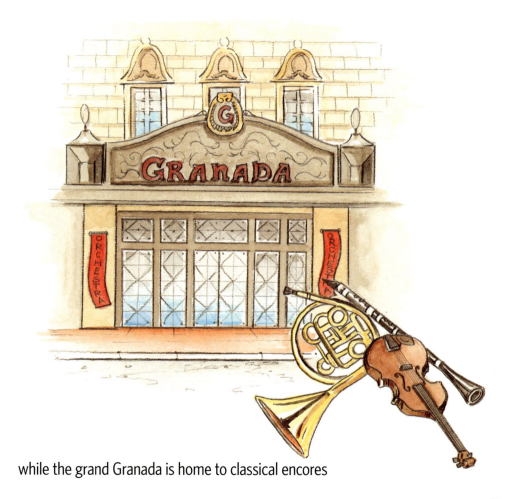

while the grand Granada is home to classical encores

The show goes on with movies and music at the 1931 Arlington Theatre

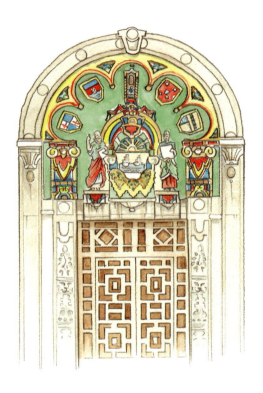

The Museum of Art and the Public Library open doors
to the beauty of fine art and knowledge

I Madonnari Festival colors Old Mission Santa Barbara with a rainbow of chalk

Happy memories made at El Encanto...

and warm moments fireside at San Ysidro Ranch

Colorful bougainvillea rolls out the red carpet in charming Summerland

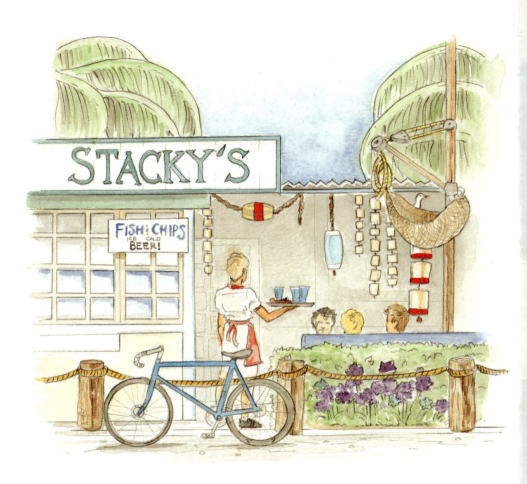

Antique finds and nautical shacks invite
the curious and the discriminating to seek and shop Summerland

The quaint lower village of Montecito
is dotted with shops and cafes...

while an adobe church leads
the way to the upper village

Secret gardens of Lotusland bloom in magical surroundings...

as classical repertoire takes center stage at the Music Academy of the West

Escape California style at the timeless Biltmore and Coral Casino

Sunset sails and harborside cocktails serve up a perfect ending to any day

Horsing around is a local pastime at polo matches and the rodeo

Sunday in the park means a walk with art

Painted ponies on a 1916 carousel
delight all ages at Chase Palm Park

Fresh from local fields comes a bounty at Old Town Farmers Market

Summer Solstice parade leads revelers to Alameda Park and fun in the sun

The painted ladies of Brinkerhoff Avenue share a cherished past

Giraffes at the zoo, octopuses at the sea center, butterflies at the botanical gardens and a hungry T-Rex at the natural history museum...

...oh my!

Rock paintings by the Chumash Indians tell the story of a prehistoric people

San Marcos Pass bridges the gap between the past and the present

154

A stagecoach delivers a touch of the old west in Santa Ynez

Los Olivos — a spot for sundries
and sipping local wines in a quartet of Adirondacks

As fall colors turn on the vine...

Windmills and Danish pastries are served up as welcome wagons in Solvang

Anacapa

Island Fox and Arch Rock are familiar tenants of the scenic Channel Islands

San Nicolas   Santa Barbara

Storke Tower — a beacon at UCSB's seaside campus and lagoon

Winter's holiday Parade of Lights illuminates sea and sky over Santa Barbara

With thanks

For both of us, this book would not have happened without the love and support of so many friends and family who constantly keep us buoyed in both calm and rough waters. We offer heartfelt thanks to David Craddock and Linda Wenglikowski, two for the road who share our fondness for the red tile city by the sea; to Steve Smith, our ever-vigilant business manager who also keeps us laughing along the way; and to Andrew Katnik, as efficient an assistant as one would ever hope to find.

Bringing this book to fruition was in large part due to the talents of more than a few gifted minds, with special thanks to Patricia LaVigne for her constant encouragement and suggestions for all things creative; and to Linda Warren and her talented colleagues at the Warren Group, whose collective eye for design is always beautifully expressed on these pages.

We thank you all from the bottom of our hearts.

About the writer

Jane Centofante worked as a magazine editor before taking up life as a freelance editor of non-fiction books. Her first book in this coastal series was *Manhattan Beach: A California Beach Town.* She and her husband were married in Santa Barbara and always return... same time, next year.

About the artist

Mike West is from just about everywhere but eventually settled in the Los Angeles area and attended the Art Center College of Design in Pasadena. He frequently visits Santa Barbara for one festival or another.